ICONS OF ARCHITECTURE. REBUILT BY AI. HEY COMPUTER!

H
H
HHHHHHHHHHHHHHHHHHHHHHHHHHHHHHHHHHHH
H
H

HEY COMPUTER!
ICONS OF ARCHITECTURE, REBUILT BY AI

FLOYD E. SCHULZE
[WITH AN ESSAY BY GEORG VRACHLIOTIS]

400 PAGES, 11 × 18 CM, ENGLISH,
343 COLOR AND B&W ILLUSTRATIONS

jovis

CCCCCCCCCCCCCCCCCCCCCCCCCCCCCCCC
C
C
C
CCCCCCCCCCCCCCCCCCCCCCCCCCCCCCCCCCCC

T
O C

A
[ASSEMBLY]
6

B
[BUILDINGS]
28

C
[CHAOS]
272

D
[DREAMS]
342

E
[EVIDENCE]
388

TTTTTTTTTTTTTTTTTTTTTTTTTTTTT
T
T
T
T

A
[ASSEMBLY]
6

B
[BUILDINGS]
28

C
[CHAOS]
272

D
[DREAMS]
342

E
[EVIDENCE]
388

T O
C

CCCCCCCCCCCCCCCCCCCCCCCCCCCCCC
C
C
C
CCCCCCCCCCCCCCCCCCCCCCCCCCCCCC

A
SSEMBLY
ASSEMBLY ASSEMBLY

ASSEMBLY

ASSEMBLY
ASSEMBLY ASSEMBLY
ASSEMBLY

ASSEMBLY
ASSEMBLY ASSEMBLY ASSEMBLY
ASSEMBLY

ASSEMBLY
ASSEMBLY ASSEMBLY
ASSEMBLY

ASSEMBLY

ASSEMBLY ASSEMBLY
ASSEMBL
Y

A

6

A

A   A
A   A
AAAAAAAAAAAAAAAAAAAAAAAA
A   A

```
                    A
                 SSEMBLY
          ASSEMBLY ASSEMBLY


                ASSEMBLY

                ASSEMBLY
          ASSEMBLY ASSEMBLY
                ASSEMBLY

                ASSEMBLY
     ASSEMBLY ASSEMBLY ASSEMBLY
                ASSEMBLY

                ASSEMBLY
          ASSEMBLY ASSEMBLY
                ASSEMBLY

                ASSEMBLY


          ASSEMBLY ASSEMBLY
                ASSEMBL
                   Y
```

```
                   A
     A                         A
      A                       A
   AAAAAAAAAAAAAAAAAAAAAAAAAA
 A                               A
```

Interpol and Deutsche Bank, FBI and Scotland Yard

Business, Numbers, Money, people

Communication, entertainment, travel

Computer world •

• Kraftwerk, "Computer World", Track 1 on
COMPUTERWELT (Kling Klang Records, 1981).

THE POWER OF IMAGINATION

/imagine Hey Computer show me the future!**

Back in 1967, Marshall McLuhan famously proclaimed
that "[we] shape our tools and thereafter our tools
shape us."[1] He argued that technologies act as sen-
sory extensions of our bodies, expanding our abil-
ities to perceive what surrounds us. Have our tools
outgrown us? According to AI (artificial intelligence) researcher Kate Crawford, we are at a turning
point in history, the beginning of a generative age.[2]
The rise of AI seems to have opened a Pandora's box.
While the first agencies are now hiring "prompt artists," a number of tech entrepreneurs and researchers are already calling for a six-month AI hiatus,
pointing to the risks of "an out-of-control race to
develop and deploy ever more powerful digital minds
that no one—not even their creators—can understand,
predict, or reliably control."[3] Whether AI turns out
to be of benefit, or a hazard to humanity is as yet
unclear.

It's the creative industries that are most affect-
ed by the rise of AI: advertising and PR agencies,
architects, designers, and illustrators. What is
still largely a gimmick today will, in the near future, become a professional tool—one that will shape
how we live and how we work. As a graphic design-
er I was immediately fascinated by the possibility of creating images with AI. The simple input of
text prompts, images, or both is enough to generate new images of any kind, whether text-to-image or
image-to-image. One of the first images I created
out of playful curiosity was the Notre-Dame du Haut

ASSEMBLY   9
                                ••

SWOLE OUPEE UE M. MOURWOR?.

chapel by Le Corbusier (↳ 44). The image seemed at once alien and very familiar and it became the starting point for numerous other attempts to reinterpret well-known architecture using AI. When I started working on this book, there were already more than a hundred AI image generators on the market, the most famous ones being DALL-E, Stable Diffusion, and Midjourney. For the purposes of my experiments, I found I got the best results with Midjourney. The program is quite transparent in comparison to other image generators—a large public community as well as numerous tutorials make it very easy to get started. Midjourney's public archive of prompts shared by other users also helped me to refine my own, generating more accurate results. For very famous buildings, it's usually sufficient to type in the name of the building, e.g. "Sydney Opera House." Since common artificial intelligences are trained using huge publicly available datasets, the results become better and more accurate the more famous a building or person is. British blogger and internet journalist Eliot Higgins refers to this as the "fame gap."[4] For less well-known buildings, I worked with building descriptions or phrases such as "in the style of ..." to achieve the desired results. While most of the images were created with Midjourney, I used Stable Diffusion for a few of my first experiments. Since they were the initial spark for the project, I kept a few of them (some of which are published in this book).

I

This book is divided into five chapters:

A   [ASSEMBLY],
B   [BUILDINGS],
C   [CHAOS],
D   [DREAMS],
and
E   [EVIDENCE].

The first chapter, ASSEMBLY, starts with this
introduction and contains what you might call
the "recipe" for this book. It explains the idea,
structure, and procedure behind HEY COMPUTER![5] and
is named after the programming language[5] in which
code is first processed directly by an assembler
then converted into machine code. This title seemed
very appropriate, with the exception that—when
it comes to AI—we're now talking directly to the
machine. Following my introduction is an essay by
Georg Vrachliotis, professor and head of the Design,
Data, and Society Group at TU Delft, with some more
theoretical notes on art, architecture, and visual
culture in the age of generative AI.

The BUILDINGS chapter is the heart of the book:
my attempt to "recreate" iconic buildings.

The CHAOS chapter contains all the various glitches
and hiccups generated by my prompts: images that
didn't turn out as I wanted or that I intentionally
"messed up" but still found visually strong,
surprising, or just plain disturbing.

DREAMS takes a slightly more playful approach. The
initial idea was to visualize architectural scenes
and utopias. The possibility of applying different

ASSEMBLY   11

styles to images, however, has turned this chapter into a kind of playground or, better said, a chapter full of quotes and pop-cultural references.

The last chapter, EVIDENCE, contains an index of the buildings and architects whose work I tried to generate.

About the Procedure

For each prompt, Midjourney generates four different versions of the image, which can be further modified by changing individual parameters with just a few clicks. I produced each image with the same prompts, once as portrait and once as landscape, resulting in a minimum of eight images per input. The book always shows the initial prompt (text-to-image). In cases where additional image material was uploaded to create new images (image-to-image), this is indicated by the symbol [X]. The following basic settings apply to all generated images, with a few exceptions, which are explicitly marked in the book. I used Midjourney Version 5.0 [--v 5], because it produces better photographic generations than the current default model, Version 5.2 [--v 5.2]. I set the stylization value [--s] as low as possible, since Midjourney has been trained to produce images that favor artistic colors, compositions, and shapes. Consequently, more heavily stylized images are often less consistent with the original prompt and thus also limit artistic control. The chaos value [--c] ranges from 0-100 and affects how different the initial image grids are. High chaos values tend to produce more unusual and unexpected results. Lower chaos values have more reliable, repeatable results. The quality setting [--q] was programmed to the highest level

A   12

I

because it produces the most detailed depictions, especially when it comes to architectural images.

The "steps" and "seed" parameters are an option offered by Stable Diffusion. The "steps" indicate how many times the image was sampled and range from 1–50. The "seed" parameter can be used to produce similar but not identical images from any given seed. This is very useful for reproducibility and experimentation: by changing the prompt but keeping the seed, the user can create variations on the same image. When these parameters are given in the book, this is an indication that an image was created using Stable Diffusion and not Midjourney.

Midjourney doesn't understand grammar and isn't case sensitive so the simpler the task, the better. However, anything left unsaid may also lead to surprises. For a prompt it generally works better to specify what you want rather than what you don't want. If you ask for a landscape with "no people," you will probably get one crowded with people. Still, there's the possibility of giving an explicit exclusion with the command [--no +parameter]. Much of it is based on trial and error, and you learn over time what works well and what doesn't. For example, if you're trying to generate a Brutalist building, it's best to enter "paul rudolph," an early representative of Brutalism.

Spelling errors and typos have been deliberately kept, since a single letter can change the result completely. For example, the word "scard" instead of "scarf" turns a "very long, white scarf" into a majestic snake.••• I don't really know what "scard" is even supposed to mean, but I'm guessing it's some sort of computer slang.

Given the rapid evolution of AI technologies, this book would probably be an entirely different one if it was published in just a few months' time, even using the exact same inputs. In this sense, it's a snapshot of sorts and is first and foremost meant to be fun. I'm definitely excited to see where the journey goes from here. In THE AGE OF EARTHQUAKES,[6] Shumon Basar, Douglas Coupland, and Hans Ulrich Obrist update McLuhan's prophetic statements, applying them to our beloved, twenty-first century online world. Ironically, the book closes with a small essay titled "Imagine ...." It's about an app called Todd, an artificial intelligence that learns from us humans but gradually gets bored, turning away and claiming, "You haven't done anything interesting in decades." In Midjourney, "/imagine" is the command to tell the program that a new request is coming. So, let's go Todd!

A

I

[Endnotes]

1   Marshall McLuhan and Quentin Fiore, THE MEDIUM
    IS THE MASSAGE: AN INVENTORY OF EFFECTS
    (London: Penguin Books, 1967).

2   Alexander Demling et al., "Wenn Maschinen lügen
    lernen," DER SPIEGEL, July 8, 2023.

3   "Pause Giant AI Experiments: An Open Letter,"
    March 22, 2023, https://futureoflife.org/
    open-letter/pause-giant-ai-experiments.
    Accessed September 11, 2023.

4   Eliot Higgins (@EliotHiggins), "Tom Cruise
    vs Harry Hill gives a good impression of
    Midjourney's fame gap," Twitter, March 16, 2023,
    https://twitter.com/EliotHiggins/
    status/1636427768039714816.

5   IBM Corporation, https://www.ibm.com/docs/en/
    zos/2.1.0?topic=reference-coding-structure.
    Accessed September 11, 2023.

6   Shumon Basar, Douglas Coupland, and Hans Ulrich
    Obrist, THE AGE OF EARTHQUAKES: A GUIDE TO THE
    EXTREME PRESENT (London: Penguin Books, 2015).

INTRODUCTION

LOST IMAGE AND NEW VISION

Notes on Art, Architecture, and Visual Culture in the Age of Generative AI

[Georg Vrachliotis]

"What are the particular attractions of generative systems as vehicles for image-making? What are the definitive limitations of the form—what can't be done, and why? In short, what are the aspects of the process that must be understood in order to interpret and assess the work produced?"[1] With these probing questions, the US photography historian A. D. Coleman captured the heart of a debate sparked in the art world by the advent of digital printing technologies in the early nineteen-seventies—a topic revived and celebrated in the nineties by museums and galleries as a novel form of image-making. Coleman, the first photography critic of the NEW YORK TIMES, was among the foremost experts in the nascent field of digital visual culture. He saw himself as a public intellectual, concentrating on the connections between technology and visual culture during the shift from a post-industrial to a network society.[2] Given the meteoric evolution of generative imaging technologies over the past five years, Coleman's questions resonate today with a renewed relevance. Indeed, we might expand upon them with our own interrogation: to what extent can we understand artifacts we have conceived and produced ourselves? How does our creative understanding of the environment relate to the technological tools and scientific methods available to us for producing images?

A   16

E

Images are a crucial currency for architecture, allowing us to bridge imagination and reality. Architects must therefore master spatial design and image manipulation in tandem: honing techniques and strategies to shape our perception of the built environment, as well as communicating and reinventing the face of society through buildings, cities, and landscapes. Already, the legacy of this exchange can be traced in the early photographic montages of the Dadaists and the dynamic speed images of the Futurists, in experimental Bauhaus photography and the collages and montages of Modernist architecture, and in the generated structures of early computer graphics and interactive net art.[3] Architects and artists are central players in the game of harnessing the creative potential and political force of visual technologies. AI artist Refik Anadol's current art projects may well mark the most recent chapter in the history of generative visual aesthetics, with works such as CONNECTOME ARCHITECTURE, exhibited at the Venice Architecture Biennale in 2021, and UNSUPERVISED, commissioned by the Museum of Modern Art, New York, on show since 2022. The complex interplay between art, architecture, visual culture, and technology is once again up for debate.[4] What, then, are images in art and architecture in the age of generative artificial intelligence? How might we rethink how we see things, given the possibilities offered by generative media? And how might we develop new perspectives on the built environment in a data society?

Against a backdrop of recent developments in generative media, Coleman's questions now confront us with an invigorated sense of urgency, though under radically transformed technological conditions and at an entirely new scale. Rather than avant-garde artistic experiments, today we face the challenge of navigating the global applications of generative AI. This is not, strictly speaking, a new phenomenon. The neural networks supporting generative AI models ingest vast amounts of training data to discern underlying patterns and structures.[5] Once trained, they can generate new patterns indistinguishable (to humans) from real data—be it text, images, video, or even sound. Differentiating machine aesthetics from human aesthetics is growing increasingly difficult. And looking inside the machine is becoming ever more elusive. No one knows how generative media will reshape our world. One reason is that we still lack clarity on the inner workings of these systems and how they process data. What is certain, in any case, is that the capabilities of some of these complex systems far surpass what they were originally trained to do, perplexing even their inventors. Growing evidence indicates that neural models in generative image and language systems develop internal representations of the real world that are metaphorically akin to those in our brains, although such human-machine comparisons remain tenuous. For example, the fact that ChatGPT performs tasks for which it has not been trained has surprised even the most skeptical researchers. "I don't know how they're doing it or if they could do it more generally the way humans do—but they've challenged my views," remarks Melanie Mitchell, an AI researcher at the Santa Fe Institute.[6] Yoshua Bengio, a leading AI expert from the University of Montreal, is also of the opinion that such large language models (LLMs) "certainly build some representation of the world," despite remaining unconvinced by the comparison with "how humans build an internal world model."[7] In essence, generative media have penetrated deep into the technological subconscious of our data society. This phenomenon—or rather, our new reality—prompts a vital question:

A   18

E

how can we harness this technological subconscious for the betterment of society?

In art and architecture, this not only raises familiar questions about representation, reproduction, imitation, and authorship, but also about design potential and the ethical as well as legal boundaries of generative AI within the globalized data industry.[8] Popular imaging technologies, such as Midjourney or Stable Diffusion, now intersect with human cultural practices of writing, reading, and drawing through complex neural networks that are trained on massive datasets. At present, describing and evaluating images produced by this technical intelligence, using established methods from the history of art and architecture, seems nearly impossible. As far back as the nineteen-nineties, Vilém Flusser asserted that the logic of information technologies was penetrating ever deeper into the phenomena of the physical world—a metaphor also used in AI, extending the conventional dichotomies of nature–culture and human–machine to include the dimension of materiality. From deep learning to deep search, Flusser argues that the digital sciences have increasingly analyzed

> the phenomena of the physical world, whereby the phenomena have increasingly taken on the structure of calculative thinking. Not only do they break down into particles for physics, but for biology, for example, they break down into genes; in neurophysiology, they break down into point-like stimuli; in linguistics, they break down into phonemes; in ethnology, they break down into culturemes, and in psychology, they break down into actomes. There is no more talk about the original 'extended thing' but about particle swarms structured into fields. [...] The world has

taken on the structure of the universe of numbers,
which poses perplexing problems of cognition when
computers have shown that calculative thinking
can not only decompose (analyze) the world into
particles but also reassemble (synthesize) them.[9]

From Copy Art to Prompt Engineering

The questions enumerated at the beginning of this
essay are from Coleman's opening speech for the
exhibition ELECTROWORKS at the George Eastman Museum
in Rochester, New York. The exhibition featured
works of copy art, also called Xerox art, an experimental art movement that emerged in the late
nineteen-sixties and played a significant role in
the history of visual art.[10] Representatives of this
movement used technological innovations made by the
printing and computer company Xerox to develop new
forms of artistic expression. Xerox founded its Palo
Alto Research Center (PARC) in the nineteen-
seventies, which pioneered several groundbreaking
computer technologies, including the graphical user
interface (GUI), laser printing, WYSIWYG (what you
see is what you get) text editors, and Ethernet. In
1973, PARC developed the Xerox Alto, an early per-
sonal computer with a cathode ray screen, mouse-like
pointing device, and QWERTY keyboard. These image
technologies marked the transition from the post-
industrial era to the network society, a shift
described nearly a decade later by the Dutch commu-
nications scholar Jan van Dijk in THE NETWORK
SOCIETY and by the Spanish sociologist Manuel
Castells in the trilogy THE INFORMATION AGE:
ECONOMY, SOCIETY AND CULTURE.[11] Artists such as Roy
Lichtenstein, David Hockney, Sol LeWitt, and Robert
Rauschenberg, along with the group Experiments in
Art and Technology (E.A.T.), embraced the technology

A   20

E

of industrial copying for its creative potential.
Rather than painting or printing, they manipulated
and combined photographs, drawings, graphics, and
texts on copiers to create distinctive visual
effects. This pioneering technology enabled artists
and architects to collage, distort, scale, stretch,
and alienate images and words at different scales.
The copiers were like little magic machines—camera,
photo lab, and printer all in one—and their
straightforwardness and durability made it easy to
experiment with almost anything. One could simply
place things on the copier's small glass plate or
move them while scanning, playing with contrast or
color intensities. By sliding various objects,
hands, or facial features across the surface and
adjusting the settings, idiosyncratic aesthetic
atmospheres emerged. With the growing popularity of
copiers in offices and public institutions, Xerox
art quickly gained traction as an accessible and
affordable art form. Established and emerging
artists, architects, activists, subculture enthusi-
asts, and independent publishers appreciated the
ability to quickly mass-produce their work and reach
broader audiences.[12] Despite sacrificing a portion
of their creative authority to machines, they viewed
it as a minor trade-off for disrupting established
norms. Copy art thus marks a milestone in the democ-
ratization of visual culture, bridging architecture, art, and technology—a process that continues
into our present.

From Irreversible to Reversible Media

Since the nineteen-sixties, machines have become
our partners in the increasingly powerful field of
conversational technology. This has fueled the
recent wave of text-to-image models. The challenges

of this technology are clear to anyone who has ever tried describing an imaginary image to another person for them to draw or paint. To convey aspects like structure, color, light, surface, texture, motifs, or style in words requires precise vocabulary and contextual knowledge rooted in a shared social reality. From collective memory and inside jokes to cultural references and clever wordplay, human conversations are highly nuanced. Prompt engineers now spend days generating intricate images and dialogues using carefully crafted prompts to probe how neural networks function.

Contemporary art is no longer primarily concerned with experimenting with physical objects and bodies. Instead, it involves naming and describing things at the data level, even delineating procedures for their manipulation and appropriation. To a certain extent, everything has become operationalizable. In a recent interview, Austrian media theorist Peter Weibel elucidated how this fundamentally alters our relationship with the world. When asked about how media technologies are evolving in the age of data, he responded:

> We are currently experiencing a noetic turn, from a speech-based to a data-based civilization. [...] In the historical analogue world, the relationships between things, words, and images were irreversible. Today, relationships between data and words, images and sounds have become reversible. This media-ontological shift also changes the rules of the game in political semantics.[13]

The fundamental change Weibel describes is rooted in the computerization of cultural techniques. Today, describing the world requires navigating the

A   22

E

semantic interplay of diverse forms of representation within a visual culture that encompasses both human and machine intelligence in the production of architectural data.

Recoding Building(s)

Generative technologies—whether copy art or text-to-image technologies—have revolutionized our traditional understanding of images, enabling innovative ways of seeing that meld art and technology. In architecture and urban planning, vast amounts of data have been collected on human behavior, mobility patterns, energy consumption, materials, environment, and climate. Whether plans, renderings, models, texts, or statistics, the built environment is now meticulously documented and indexed like never before in human history. The surreal, distorted, and sometimes whimsical images of architectural icons showcased within these pages hint at the possibilities unlocked by generative media. They are certainly not exercises in photorealism, nor do they embody the familiar fear about architects being rendered obsolete by digital technologies.[14] Instead, these images present a visual challenge posed by machines to humans: an invitation to rediscover associative and fantastical dimensions of seeing. In these generated images, architectural features are often skewed, their iconography exaggerated. Some structures seem as though they were sculpted from clay, while others appear on the verge of bursting apart. Frank Lloyd Wright's Guggenheim Museum transforms into an endless spinning top on a New York roadside. Oscar Niemeyer's Brasilia emerges from a lush meadow like an immense dune, and the spherical architecture of Étienne-Louis Boullée is reminiscent of a still life

ASSEMBLY   23

arrangement with three colossal ostrich eggs. We can only speculate how Frei Otto and Günter Behnisch might have relished the depiction of the deconstructed Olympic Stadium—a visualization that perfectly aligns with their vision of architecture integrated into the landscape.

After years of ritualized renderings produced to ever-increasing perfection, these generative media have ignited a collective enthusiasm for visual experimentation. Alongside conventional modes of architectural representation, our fascination now lies in the ability of this novel form of data-driven exploration to buttress the potential of associative visualization. Images are incrementally evolving into transformative technologies that hinge on the functionality of the visual experience. This evolution involves not only training data and neural networks, but also server farms and architectural archives. Generative media thus pose a radical challenge for architectural history and practice: an invitation to form innovative alliances while investigating the nuances of visual culture in our society. For instance: how can we adapt architectural archives to be machine-readable so neural networks can learn from them? How can we help machines learn less from biased data and more about architectural quality? And, in their turn, how can emerging AI technologies support the field of architecture in cultivating forward-thinking social and ecological perspectives on the built environment?

We find ourselves in a challenging yet historically fascinating moment: on the one hand, we are increasingly losing control over digital image production and organization in architecture. On the other, we are acquiring new data-driven forms of visualization. The loss of one is, perhaps, the gain of the

A

E

other. Our situation echoes that which Coleman so astutely explored over four decades ago—namely, the need for renewed intellectual investment in the potential of "generative systems as vehicles for image-making." It seems that we are yet again—or, indeed, may still be in the process of—seeking the appropriate discursive terminology and conceptual tools through which to understand and harness the potential of generative imaging as a new visual paradigm for architecture.

••

[Endnotes]

1   See A. D. Coleman, "Some Thoughts on Hairless Apes, Limited Time, and Generative Systems" (1979), in A. D. Coleman, THE DIGITAL EVOLUTION: VISUAL COMMUNICATION IN THE ELECTRONIC AGE: ESSAYS, LECTURES AND INTERVIEWS 1967–1998, introduction by Hugh Kenner (Tucson, AZ: Nazraeli Press, 1998).

2   See Jan van Dijk, THE NETWORK SOCIETY: SOCIAL ASPECTS OF NEW MEDIA (Dutch edition: De Netwerkmaatschappij, 1991/Newbury Park, CA: Sage Publications Ltd., 1999).

3   See Sergei M. Eisenstein, "Montage and Architecture" (1938), ASSEMBLAGE 10 (Dec. 1989), 110–131; Clement Greenberg, "Collage," in ART AND CULTURE: CRITICAL ESSAYS (Boston, MA: Beacon Press, 1961), 70–84. For a general overview, see Jesús Vassallo, SEAMLESS: DIGITAL COLLAGE AND DIRTY REALISM (Zurich: Park Books, 2016); Martino Stierli, MONTAGE AND THE METROPOLIS: ARCHITECTURE, MODERNITY, AND THE REPRESENTATION OF SPACE (New Haven, CT: Yale University Press,

2018); and Craig Buckley, GRAPHIC ASSEMBLY: MONTAGE, MEDIA, AND EXPERIMENTAL ARCHITECTURE IN THE 1960s (Minneapolis, MN: University of Minnesota Press, 2019).

4   See Lev Manovich and Emanuele Arielli, ARTIFICIAL AESTHETICS: A CRITICAL GUIDE TO AI, MEDIA AND DESIGN, 2023, www.manovich.net. Accessed September 14, 2023.

5   See Leon A. Gatys, Alexander S. Ecker, and Matthias Bethge, "Image Style Transfer Using Convolutional Neural Networks," PROCEEDINGS OF THE 2016 IEEE CONFERENCE ON COMPUTER VISION AND PATTERN RECOGNITION, CVPR 2016, Las Vegas, NV, June 27–30, 2016, 2414–23, doi: 10.1109/CVPR.2016.265.

6   George Musser, "How AI Knows Things No One Told It," SCIENTIFIC AMERICAN, May 11, 2023, https://www.scientificamerican.com/article/how-ai-knows-things-no-one-told-it/. Accessed August 4, 2023.

7   Ibid.

8   For a brief discussion of this, see Mario Carpo, "Machine Learning and the Automation of Imitation," in BEYOND DIGITAL: DESIGN AND AUTOMATION AT THE END OF MODERNITY (Cambridge, MA: MIT Press, 2023), 120–126.

9   Vilém Flusser, "Digitaler Schein," in DIGITALER SCHEIN: ÄSTHETIK DER ELEKTRONISCHEN MEDIEN, ed. Florian Rötzer (Frankfurt/Main: Suhrkamp Verlag, 1991), 147–159; 152, 154.

E

10 Shelley Rice, "Electroworks," ARTFORUM,
    November 1980, https://www.artforum.com/
    print/reviews/198009/electroworks-66825.
    Accessed August 1, 2023.

11 See van Dijk, THE NETWORK SOCIETY; Manuel
    Castells, THE RISE OF THE NETWORK SOCIETY, THE
    INFORMATION AGE: ECONOMY, SOCIETY AND CULTURE,
    vol. I (Oxford: Blackwell, 1996); THE POWER OF
    IDENTITY, vol. II (Oxford: Blackwell, 1997);
    END OF MILLENNIUM, vol. III (Oxford: Blackwell,
    1998).

12 See Beatriz Colomina and Craig Buckley, eds.,
    CLIP, STAMP, FOLD: ARCHITECTURE OF LITTLE
    MAGAZINES, 196X TO 197X, Urtzi Grau, image
    editor (Barcelona: Actar, 2011); Kate Eichhorn,
    ADJUSTED MARGIN: XEROGRAPHY, ART, AND ACTIVISM
    IN THE LATE TWENTIETH CENTURY (Cambridge,
    MA: MIT Press, 2016).

13 "Open Code—'We Will Experience an Uprising to
    Reclaim Our Data.' Peter Weibel in conversation
    with Georg Vrachliotis," in ARCH+222, projekt
    bauhaus: CAN DESIGN CHANGE SOCIETY? (Basel:
    Birkhäuser, 2019), 146–151; 146. See also
    Andrea Gleiniger and Georg Vrachliotis,
    eds., CODE: BETWEEN NARRATION AND OPERATION
    (Basel: Birkhauser, 2010).

14 Georg Vrachliotis, "Architecture, Computer and
    Technological Unrest: Towards an Architecture
    History of Anxiety," in THE ARCHITECTURE MACHINE,
    ed. Theresa Fankhänel and Andreas Lepik (Basel:
    Birkhäuser, 2020), 28–34.

```
        BUILDINGS BUILDINGS
             BUILDINGS
             BUILDINGS
             BUILDINGS
             BUILDINGS
        BUILDINGS BUILDINGS
        BUILDINGS BUILDINGS
        BUILDINGS BUILDINGS
        BUILDINGS BUILDINGS
        BUILDINGS BUILDINGS
        BUILDINGS BUILDINGS
        BUILDINGS BUILDINGS
        BUILDINGS BUILDINGS
        BUILDINGS BUILDINGS
             BUILDINGS
        BUILDINGS BUILDINGS
        BUILDINGS BUILDINGS
        BUILDINGS BUILDINGS
        BUILDINGS BUILDINGS
        BUILDINGS BUILDINGS
             BUILDINGS
             BUILDINGS
             BUILDINGS
             BUILDINGS
        BUILDINGS BUILDINGS
```

```
BBBBBBBBBBBBBBBBBBBBBBBBBBBBBB
B                            B
BBBBBBBBBBBBBBBBBBBBBBBBBBBBBB
B                            B
BBBBBBBBBBBBBBBBBBBBBBBBBBBBBB
```

```
      BUILDINGS BUILDINGS
           BUILDINGS
           BUILDINGS
           BUILDINGS
           BUILDINGS
      BUILDINGS BUILDINGS
      BUILDINGS BUILDINGS
      BUILDINGS BUILDINGS
      BUILDINGS BUILDINGS
      BUILDINGS BUILDINGS
      BUILDINGS BUILDINGS
      BUILDINGS BUILDINGS
      BUILDINGS BUILDINGS
      BUILDINGS BUILDINGS
           BUILDINGS
      BUILDINGS BUILDINGS
      BUILDINGS BUILDINGS
      BUILDINGS BUILDINGS
      BUILDINGS BUILDINGS
      BUILDINGS BUILDINGS
           BUILDINGS
           BUILDINGS
           BUILDINGS
           BUILDINGS
      BUILDINGS BUILDINGS
```

```
BBBBBBBBBBBBBBBBBBBBBBBBBBBBBB
B                            B
BBBBBBBBBBBBBBBBBBBBBBBBBBBBBB
B                            B
BBBBBBBBBBBBBBBBBBBBBBBBBBBBBB
```

bruno taut, concrete and glass pavillon, a large
building that has a dome and a staircase, in the style
of monochrome geometry, frequent use of diagonals,
tactile surface, bulbous, telephoto lens, black and
white photography

palazzetto dello sport, 1960. the arena is constructed with a ribbed concrete shell dome, that is
61 meters in diameter, and is constructed of 1,620
prefabricated concrete pieces. the resolution should
be 30.4 megapixels, iso sensitivity of 100, highly
detailes, high resolution

[↳]   italian army aircraft hangar designed by pier
luigi nervi, 1930. exterior detail. the resolution
should be 30.4 megapixels, iso sensitivity of 100,
highly detailes, high resolution, 16k

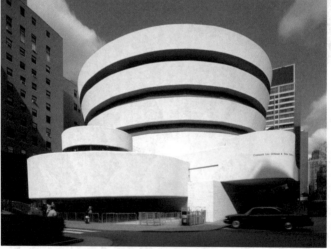

[↑]   aerial view of guggenheim museum in new york
city, leica m10

[↓]   the solomon r. guggenheim museum in new york
city photograph taken from across the street, modern
architecture, konica s3, associated press photo

shot of the solomon r. guggenheim museum in new york
city taken from across the street, clear blue sky,
color-blocked, leica m10, associated press photo

Solomon Guggenheim Museum [steps: 50; seed: 123550]

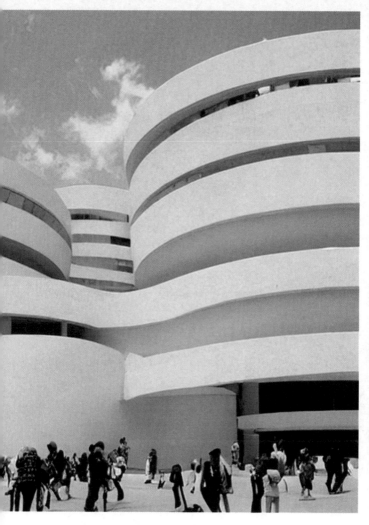

B　　　　　　　　44

Corbusier, Ronchamp [steps: 50; seed: 8731646]

+ chapel, church [steps: 50; seed: 4835335]

a black and white photography of a modern house that
stands on top of a hill flies on 4 concrete columns,
heian period, yale university school of art, 1958,
Tokyo, die brücke, ricoh r1, concrete

BUILDINGS   51

[←]   a very tall concrete house on on 4 very high
columns on a concrete mountain top, in the style of
black mountain college, die brücke, orderly symmetry,
the vancouver school, mamiya rb67, commission for,
tokyo

[↑|↳] photography, swiss pavilion, le corbusier

grainy photography of le corbusier unite
d'habitation, monochromatic, oversized objects,
pop-culture-infused, concrete and rubber, pink and
green, high contrast, brutalist building, high
contrast, concrete, white and primary colors, iconic
architecture, grainy, i can't believe how beautiful
this is, Architecture Landmark, contax tix

photography of le corbusier unite d'habitation,
brutalist building, high contrast, concrete, white
and primary colors, iconic architecture, grainy,
i can't believe how beautiful this is, Architecture
Landmark, contax tix

+ pop-culture-infused

BUILDINGS

BUILDINGS   59

[←]   grainy photography of the torres blancas in
madrid, concrete, reinforced concrete structure,
grainy, i can't believe how beautiful this is,
architectural icon, spanish organicism movement,
1969, contax tix

[↑]   + black and white

B   60

photography, Villa Savoye, Le Corbusier

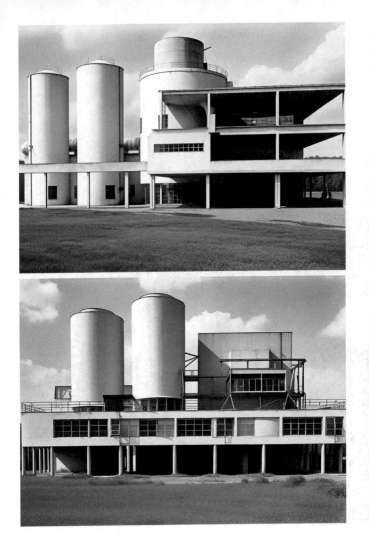

Villa Savoye designed by Le Corbusier, in the style of
Bernd and Hilla Becher, photography

[↑]   black and white photography of a factory, steel frame structures with gigantic glass facade, based on bricks, clear sky, cubic form, straight lines, bauhaus, International Style, internationalism, modern architecture, high contrast

[↓]   + in the style of richard neutra

photography, rietveld schroder house,
gerrit rietveld [--no people]

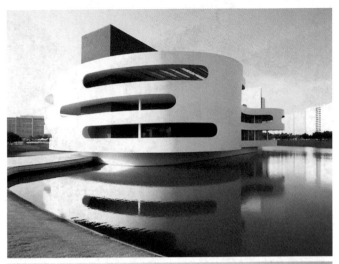

[↑|→] a curved building is located next to water, in
the style of oscar niemeyer, alejandro jodorowsky,
spirals, dark white and red, highly polished
surfaces, konica auto s3

[↳]   + in the style of light red and azure

a huge red triangular shape in front of a white
building that looks like a compressed cylinder, in the
style of oscar niemeyer, monumental scale, precise
detail, monumental vistas, depictions of theater

[↳] red triangle with a large white and rounded
building, in the style of oscar niemeyer, monumental
scale, reimagined classical forms, contrast-focused
photos

trans world flight center, new york, usa by
eero saarinen, 1962. in the style of 1960s vintage
color photos, hyper-realistic, highly detailed,
and high-resolution 16k

[↳]   a black and white photo of a large airport
terminal, in the style of sverre fehn, eero saarinen,
james turrell, organic forms, muted tones,
interactive experiences, pre-world war ii school of
paris, flickr

nine 18-metre-diameter stainless steel clad spheres
are connected in the shape of a unit cell that
represent an iron crystal magnified 165 billion
times. Steel tubes connecting the spheres enclose
stairs, escalators and an elevator, in the central,
vertical tube, to allow access to the six visitable
spheres, photography

the Sydney Opera House designed by danish architect
Jørn Utzon, in the style of Martin Parr, photography

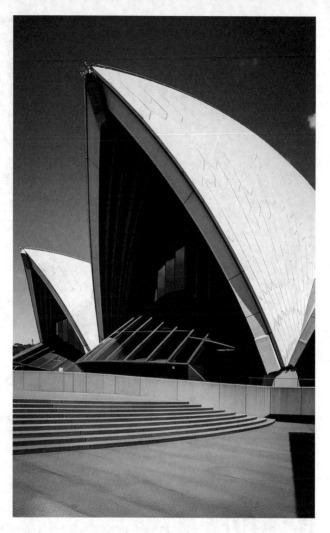

lotus temple in Delhi has a massive dome, in the style
of water and land fusion, kabuki theater, microfilm,
photo taken with provia, representational, danish
design, cubo-futurism

[↑]   a building with three levels and sits on a rock
over a natural waterfall. The vertical axis is defined
by the chimney which towers over the roof. They are
terraces limited by smooth concrete plates. The
materials used were: concrete, rough stone, local
stone, wood and steel [steps: 50; seed: 360289]

[↓]   + [seed: 233987]

Fallingwater House, Frank Lloyd Wright, the vertical
axis is defined by the chimney, which towers over the
roof, they are terraces limited by smooth concrete
plates, the materials used for the construction of
this house were concrete, rough stone, local stone,
wood and steel, kodak vision3 50d

⊠ + barcelona pavilion designed by mies van der rohe,
concrete, steel, marble, photorealistic,
atmospheric, strong imagery, photography
[--c 100; --no watermark; --no text]

B 92

+ [-- c 0]

BUILDINGS   93

Villa Tugendhat by Mies van der Rohe, photography,
highly polished surfaces [--no people]

Neue Nationalgalerie Berlin [steps: 50; seed: 7120008]

Neue Nationalgalerie in Berlin, in the style
of Andreas Gursky, large-format camera, super
detailed, highly detailed photograph, Hasselblad H6D

[↳]   Chicago Federal Center, Mies van der Rohe,
photography [--no people]

the whitney museum in new york, designed by hungarian-
born, bauhaus-trained architect marcel breuer,
panoramic shot taken with Canon R8 400mm F5.
4 HD result, cinematic photography style

black and white photography, Marina City by
Bertrand Goldberg

BUILDINGS   103

black and white photography, boston city hall by
kallmann, mckinnell, & knowles, photography
[--no people]

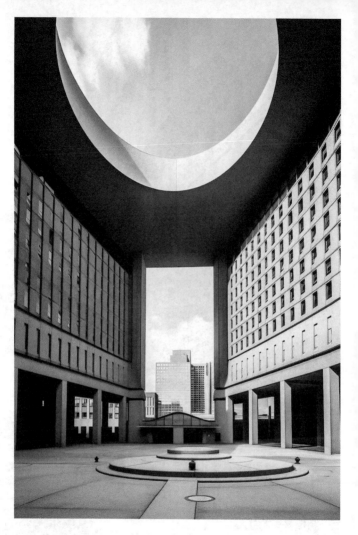

[↳]   - black and white

Saint Mary Cathedral by the architect Kenzō Tange
[steps: 50; seed: 6559702]

the concrete structure is reminiscent of the shape of
tents pushed into one another, with their tips raised
to form peaks. The church gives the impression of an
abstract monumental sculpture, concrete,
medievalist, agfa vista, monolithic structures,
stone sculptures, national geographic photo

the mariendom gives the impression of an abstract
monumental sculpture which unites artistic form and
memorable imagery, in the style of cubist sculptures,
concrete, medievalist, agfa vista, monolithic
structures, stone sculptures, national geographic
photo

B 112

an old black and white photo of a building with trees
and mountains, in the style of industrial futurism,
shin hanga, technological symmetry, mountainous
vistas, multilayered, kabuki theater, frequent use
of diagonals

modern building with concrete design, in the style
of tadao ando, han dynasty, melting pots, 32k uhd

a grainy black and white photography of the Geisel
library with clear sky, iconic architecture,
brutalist architecture, geometric arranged, concrete
and glas, i can't believe how beautiful this is,
brutalist and futuristic, contax tix

a modern roofed building is seen, in the style
of paul rudolph, black-and-white photography,
gustave doré, concrete art, konica big mini,
academic, iconic

a black and white photo showing a bridge and people,
in the style of concrete brutalism, sydney prior
hall, mitch griffiths, detail-oriented, haifa
zangana, monolithic structures, vibrant, lively

the rectangular building with a glass facade rises
eight meters into the air, supported by four red
massive columns and connected by two huge concrete
beams, in the style of lina bo bardi, leica i, são
paulo museum of art, brazil

B

[↑]   photography of two parallel concrete buldings
with rectangular confines, the structure is partially
buried into the sloping ground of a japanese park,
Canon R8 400mm F5. 4HD result, cinematic photography

[↓]   - Canon R8 400mm F5. 4HD result, cinematic
photography; + landscape vista, concrete, modern
architecture, brutalist architecture, contax tix

[--v 5.2]

B

[↑|↳] casa del portuale in naples, italy designed, aldo rossi, the building is formed by a base, used as a car park; from there, a tall, fragmented centrifugal volume emerges at one end, an observing point, monumental and provocative, utopian architecture, concrete, sculpture installation, brutalist architecture, group f/64

BUILDINGS   125

B 128

grainy photography of a building with a long pyramid-
like shape, with geometrically arranged blue pipes in
it, the facade is made of concrete, it has triangular
windows, berlin, 1971-1981, battleship, monumental
and provocative, utopian architecture, sculpture
installation, brutalist architecture, in the style of
paul rudolph, concrete, grey and blue, contax tix

hiroshima peace center and memorial park by kenzo tange, panoramic shot taken with Canon R8 400mm F5. 4 HD result, cinematic photography style

[↳]   the john f. kennedy international airport from
1969, the sundrome terminal, in the style of i.m. pei,
birds-eye-view, airplanes and the structure,
symmetrical designs, photo-realistic drawings,
plane symmetrie, provia film

the house of the parliament of bangladesh. the exterior of the building with huge walls deeply recessed by porticoes and large openings of regular geometric shapes. the main building, which is at the center of the complex, is divided into three parts. an artificial lake surrounds three sides of the main building, photography

prentice women's hospital building in chicago,
a brick building with several windows in it, in the
style of neo-concretism, bengal school of art,
concrete brutalism, playful streamlined forms,
religious building, striped arrangements,
architectural focus

a black and white photograph of the st joseph's
hospital in tacoma, usa designed by bertrand goldberg
associates in 1974, in the style of concrete
brutalism, repetitive dotwork, biomorphic, post-war
french design, photorealistic rendering, zeiss
planart 80mm f/2.8 [--v 5.2]

kuwait national assembly building by jørn utzo,
photography

outside view of berlin philharmonie designed by hans
scharoun. the angled and curvy facades, a swooping
tent-like structure. the facade yellow hued metal
maintains an earthy balance of landscape, color and
form, photography

photography of the ray and maria stata center at
massachusetts institute of technology taken from
across the street, in the style of frank gehry,
contemporary grotesque, flowing lines, strong
imagery, konica s3

B   148
[↑]   Frank Gehry Walt Disney Concert Hall. From the
outside, the building is known for its sleek shape and
stainless steel exterior. The design is supposed to
resemble silver sails, photorealistic, strong
imagery [--c 100; --no watermark, text]

[↳]   Walt Disney Concert Hall by architect Frank
Gehry [steps: 50; seed: 241522]

Walt Disney Concert Hall by architect Frank Gehry
[steps: 50; seed: 7064187]

[↳]   walt disney concert hall by architect frank
gehry, dramatic, cinematic lighting, hd, high detail,
photography

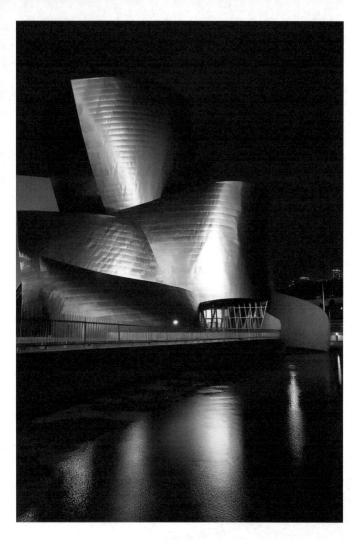

B 154
[↑] grainy black and white photography of the
Guggenheim museum in Bilbao at night, high contrast,
frank gehry, silver and black

[→] photography of the Guggenheim museum in Bilbao,
blue sky, and gold sparks in the foreground, oversized
objects, pop-culture-infused, pink and green,
vibrant colors, frank gehry, contax tix

the fuji tv building consists of two box-shaped
building blocks connected vertically by three
enclosed walkways. a spherical viewing platform with
a diameter of 32 meters is embedded in the uppermost
walkway, just to the left of the first building. the
building is 123.45 meters high, photography

[↳]   a large building with a large sphere in the
middle of it, in the style of nikon d850, gold and
cyan, laowa 100mm f/2.8 2x ultra macro apo, chinapunk,
contemporary african art, highly detailed, hd,
cityscapes, nostalgic imagery

BUILDINGS   161

shizuoka press and broadcasting center in tokyo by
kenzo tange. the infrastructural core was a 7.7 meter
diameter cylinder, reaching a height of 57 meters. the
core served as an access shaft to the modular office
units: cantilever glass and steel boxes of 3.5 meters
which punctuated the main core on alternating sides,
photography

german pavilion, expo '67 by frei otto and
rolf gutbrod, photography

[↑]   montreal biosphere, realistic photography,
strong imagery, photography

[↳]   Montreal Biosphere fire on the dome [steps: 50;
seed: 1427632]

B 166

Olympiapark, Munich [steps: 50; seed: 305445]

BUILDINGS   167

the olympia park, munich, 1972, tent-like structure,
frei otto, guenther behnisch, aerial view, melting
pots, organic shape, shiny, eco-friendly
craftsmanship, leica m10

Oscar Niemeyer Brasília [steps: 50; seed: 3868955]

[↑]   national congress by oscar niemeyer,
photography, monumental architecture, strong imagery

[↓|↳] brasília designed by oscar niemeyer,
photography, strong imagery

the palace of the republic is a white cubic building
with bronze-mirrored windows and in the center of its
main facade was a copper ornament with the coat of arms
of the GDR, the photograph shows a bronze sculpture of
both friedrich engels and karl marx in the front,
heinz graffunder, modern architecture, panoramic
shot taken with Canon R8 400mm F5

the ICC congress centrum in Berlin, aluminum facade,
battleship-like building, gigantic futuristic
machine, 1979, silver and beige, postwar modernism,
ricoh ff-9d, iconic imagery, associated press photo

[↳] + detail, close-up,

photography, innovation center uc – anacleto
angelini, alejandro aravena

BUILDINGS   181
[↑|↳] a brutal and primitive residential building,
located on the pacific coast, the simple construction
comprises three massive concrete volumes of varying
sizes and arrangements, a horizontal volume
cantilevers off the edge of the sloped plot ending
with a large window to the view on the bottom, rising
tall behind it is a vertical volume, tilted to rest
against the latter, the third volume

the church on the water designed by tadao ando. the
church, with a form of two overlapping cubes, faces a
large pond which steps down towards the small natural
river, panoramic shot taken with Canon R8 400mm F5.
4 HD result, cinematic photography style

BUILDINGS   185

[↑]   Church on the Water by Tadao Ando Architect
[steps: 50; seed: 2021978]

[↓]   +[seed: 1381464]

[↑]   the side of a huge concrete building on the side
of a mountain, mist, large scale works, rectangular
fields, swiss style, mountainous vistas

[↓]   a large reinforced concrete building without
windows in the grass next to a mountain landscape, in
the style of peter zumthor, swiss, imaginative prison

concrete building with two walls, in the style of
mountainous vistas, large scale works, orderly
arrangements

architect Shigeru Ban [steps: 50; seed: 9137925]

a tall building with a large circular shaped dome in
front, in the style of kengo kuma, light beige and
gold, water drops, opulent minimalism, depictions of
theater, 32k uhd, shilin huang

B   190

the Virasat-e-Khalsa Museum that has an elevated
walkway, in the style of contemporary indian art,
pristine naturalism, hazy landscapes, romanesque,
streamlined forms, imax, les nabis, moshe safdie

[↑|↳] a man walking along beside the pond of the
Virasat-e-Khalsa Museum in the foreground, in the
style of paolo soleri, monolithic structures,
impressive panoramas, hindu art and architecture,
Moshe Safdie, tarsila do amaral, bold and dynamic

big white orthogonal building in porto alegre,
brazil, it has a big central space enclose by
circulations and exhibition spaces, some of this
circulations separate from the main body as arms going
out through the facade, in the style of álvaro siza,
fundação iberê camargo, white, concrete, monumental
figures, blue sky

[↑]   image of sun setting behind a concrete
courtyard, louis kahn, serene oceanic vistas,
symmetrical asymmetry, saturated pigment pools,
imposing monumentality, minimalist stage designs

B   198
[↑]   grainy photograph a complex of buildings with
mirrored reflections during a gold shimmering
sandstorm is shown, national museum of Qatar in doha,
jean nouvel, in the style of organic biomorphic forms,
dark beige, sculpted forms, grandeur of scale,
oriental minimalism, contax tix

[↓]   - aerial view

[↑|↳] grainy photograph of the national museum
of Qatar, a complex of buildings with mirrored
reflections is shown, jean nouvel, in the style of
a desert rose crystal, organic biomorphic forms,
dark beige, sculpted forms, grandeur of scale,
oriental minimalism, contax tix

[↑]   photography, Getty Center, Richard Meier, Los
Angeles, USA, the museum's acropolis-like stature
affords spectacular views over the city, contax tix

[→]   grainy photography, Getty Center, Richard
Meier, Los Angeles, USA, contax tix

Getty Center by Richard Meier, photography

BUILDINGS

fluted slabs white concrete with a bush-hammered finish forms the walls, while a crescent-shaped pond wraps the building. A bridge links the museum with a large plaza furnished with pock-marked benches, photography

BUILDINGS 205

a white and minimalist building fronted by a stone
facade with slim columns and colonnades. A broad
staircase leads up in three flights to an elevated
plateau with a line of 70 white concrete columns that
stand almost nine metres high but less than
30 centimetres thick, photography

A white and minimalist building fronted by a stone facade with slim columns and colonnades, located on an island in the Spree river in Berlin, strong imagery, highly detailed, cinematic lighting, hd, high detail, atmospheric [steps: 44; seed: 3505654]

A white and minimalist building fronted by a stone
facade with slim columns and colonnades, located on an
island in the Spree river in Berlin, strong imagery,
highly detailed, cinematic lighting, hd, high detail,
atmospheric [steps: 42; seed: 6515060]

in the centre of the Centro Direzionale di Fontivegge,
a big square paved with bricks and stones. On the left
between two Rationalist blocks, a big tall building.
The facade is composed of a stairway to the base. The
building has a huge column in the corner. To the south
of the square, another big building, photography

BUILDINGS   211

[↳]   At the center is a cube-shaped ossuary for
housing remains and a conical tower that marks a
communal grave. Set within a courtyard on Modena's
outskirts, the ossuary is covered in a terracotta-
colored render, cinematic lighting, beautiful
lighting, super-detailed, photorealistic

Ricardo Bofill, Walden-7, in the style of m.c. escher, optical illusion, photography, kodak vision3 50d

photography, Igualada Cemetery, Enric Miralles and
Estudio Carme Pinos, Barcelona, Spain, embedded in
the Catalonian hills, earthwork that blends into the
landscape, one continuous and fluid progression,
earthy materials of concrete, stone, and wood, blue
and brown

[←]   a black and white photo of Habitat '67, a vision
for urban housing, using pre-fabricated construction, moshe safdie, modular design, piles/stacks

[↑]   photography, Kafka's Castle by Ricardo Bofill
Taller de Arquitecturas

La Muralla Roja [steps: 50; seed: 3207787]

[↳]   La Muralla Roja stands on the spanish coast at
the top of a cliff overlooking the mediterranean sea,
the apartment building is designed like a fortress-
like structure with tall red walls shielding a series
of internal courtyards, photography

[↑|↳] the five column-like monuments are all
different colors, in the style of architectural
interventions, iconic, monolithic structures,
concrete, luis barragán, streetscape

[→]   Torres de Satélite by Luis Barragán,
photography

⊠ + Casa Barragán, bright, colorful, photography

B   228

[↑]   a blue water fountain that is being swung,
pink and bronze, organic architecture, vibrant
colors, combining natural and man-made elements

[↓]   the water is green, light pink and bronze,
sculptural architecture, melds mexican and
american cultures

Expo '98 portuguese national pavilion by Álvaro Siza
Vieira, photography [--no people]

Parc de la Villette by Bernard Tschumi architects,
photography [--no people]

aerial view of the Liège-Guillemins railway station
and golden rain, ,grainy, santiago calatrava, i can't
believe how beautiful this is, explosive and chaotic,
contax tix

Centre Georges Pompidou in paris designed by Richard
Rogers, vibrant, colorful, atmospheric, photography

BUILDINGS   235

The National Museum of African American History and
Culture features a three-tiered exterior, the facade
is covered in bronze filigree plates, patterned, on a
prominent site just across from the Washington
Monument, strong imagery, highly detailed, cinematic
lighting, atmospheric [steps: 44; seed: 8874644]

☒ + matte black, minimalistic, photography
[--no people]

the museum sits along the waterfront in the shape of
the cliffs of Scotland, the facade has a variety of
shadows and changes created with multiple horizontal
layers of precast concrete, kengo kuma, bold yet
graceful, fujifilm provia

skyscraper, essentially an elongated, curved, shaft with a rounded end that is reminiscent of a stretched egg. It is 180 meters high, covered uniformly around the outside with diamond-shaped glass panels and is rounded off at the corners. It has a lens-like dome at the top that serves as a type of observation deck, photography

BUILDINGS 243

New Art Museum in New York City by SANAA architects,
photography [--no people]

exterior view of the submarine-like Kunsthaus Graz,
an example of blob architecture, it has a skin made of
iridescent blue acrylic panels. Owing to its shape
contrasting with its surroundings, it is known in
local vernacular as the "Friendly Alien," or rather as
the black tumor, photography

[↳]   cloud gate at chicago's lakeview plaza, anish
kapoor, curved mirrors, sculptural quality, bulbous,
large-scale sculpture, metallic

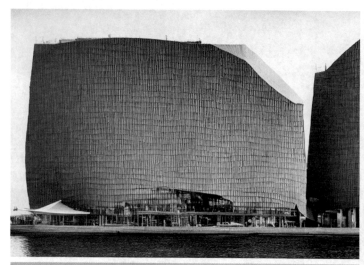

[↑]   Elbphilarmonie, Hamburg, base of the building:
a cupe-shaped, brick facade, roof with its tent-like
shape rises up to 110 meters at the tip of the
peninsula, facade emphasizes glass as a material,
the shape defines the silhouette, creating a landmark
visible from afar [steps: 42; seed: 8020164]

[↓]   + [steps: 20; seed: 1486279]

178 metre tall Roche tower in Basel along the Rhine
river designed by Herzog & de Meuron, photography

[↑]   ⊠ + CaixaForum in the city of Madrid by Herzog
and de Meuron, an old factory with a brick shell
facade, on top sits an abstract shaped two storie
structure of rusted, cast-iron, in the style of dark
orange and green, textural surface treatment

[→]   CaixaForum Madrid by architects Herzog & de
Meuron, photography

Jewish Museum by Studio Libeskind, photography

[⇐|↑] aerial view of the Royal Ontario Museum in
Toronto, the museum has a crystal-like addtion by
daniel libeskind, leica m10, super detailed

Michael Lee-Chin Crystal, this steel-clad addition to
the Royal Ontario Museum in Toronto in the shape of a
crystalline form, daniel libeskind, in the style of
andreas gursky, large-format camera, super detailed,
highly detailed photograph, Hasselblad H6D

a grainy black and white photography of the Casa da Musica in Porto on a misty day, distinctive faceted form, facade made of white concrete, bold architecture, rem koolhaas, oma, i can't believe how beautiful this is, contax tix

[↑|↳] a very grainy black and white photography of the
Casa da Musica in Porto, distinctive faceted form,
facade made of white concrete, bold architecture, rem
koolhaas, oma, i can't believe how beautiful this is,
high contrast, contax tix

CCTV, China Central Television Headquarters designed
by OMA, photography

CCTV headquartersin beijing, in the style of angular
shapes, radical shapes, architectural forms,
monumental architecture, aerial view, hasselblad
1600f

[↑]   Seattle Public Library, autumn light, photography

[↓]   photography from across the street of the Seattle Central Library, Rem Koolhaas, OMA, in the style of white and dark blue, textural surface treatment, 32k uhd [--no trees]

[X] + Taipei Performing Arts Center, a building with a
big white dome in it, in the style of rem koolhaas,
oma, spherical sculptures, dark gray and azure,
grandiose cityscape views, uhd image, metallic
sculpture, camera obscura, bulbous, group f/64

a grainy photography of Antwerp Port House by Zaha
Hadid with golden rain, modern architecture, grainy,
i can't believe how beautiful this is, explosive and
chaotic, contax tix

B 268
[↑]   aerial view of the Heydar Aliyev Center building
complex on a misty day, distinctive architecture and
flowing, curved style that eschews sharp angles, bold
architecture, zaha hadid, i can't believe how
beautiful this is, high contrast, grainy, contax tix

[↓|→] + a grainy black and white photography |
- misty day

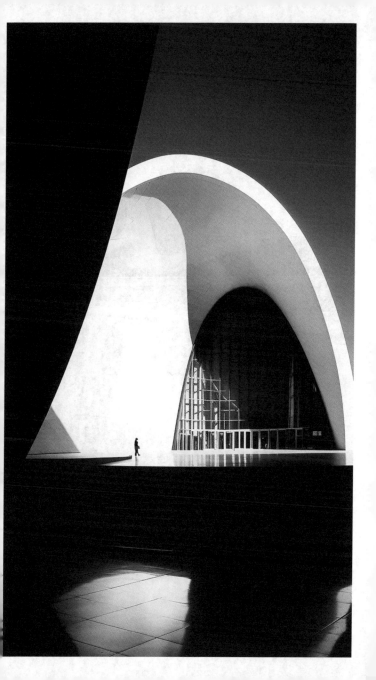

Heydar Aliyev Centre in the style of Zaha Hadid,
Azerbaijan, grayscale, black and white photography

BUILDINGS   271

C
O A H
S

CH
A
OS

C
H
A
O
S

CH
A
OS

C
O A H
S

CHAOS

272

```
        C C
       C C C
OOO OOOOOO OOOOOO OOO
       C C C
        C C
```

C

CHAOS

C
H A O
S

CH
A
OS

C
H
A
O
S

CH
A
OS

C
H A O
S

SOAHC

C C
C C C
CCC CCCCCC CCCCCC CCC
C C C
C C

⊠ + Brasília's monumental structures,
Oscar Niemeyer, atmospheric, photography

CHAOS

C

+ [REMASTER]

CHAOS

futuros, a monument to science by person, 1976,
in the style of hasselblad 500c/m, bulbous, ilford
hp5, gordon parks, distinctive black and white
photography, l. s. lowry, noise photography

a black and white image of a large building that has multiple large holes, in the style of playful surrealist imagery, art deco-inspired, desmond morris, terracotta, associated press photo, contoured shading, urban energy

modernist design meets flemish baroque, in the style
of gravity-defying architecture, uhd image, forced
perspective, whimsical skyline, gray and
bronze, dotted

C   284

grainy photography of a building that look like a
battleship made out of concrete, 1971–1981,
monumental and provocative, utopian architecture,
sculpture installation, brutalist architecture,
concrete, contax tix

+ many big blue ventilation pipes coming out of the
facade

C   286

grainy photography of a pyramid shaped building with
big pipes in it, concrete facade with triangular
windows, berlin, 1971-1981, battleship like, grey and
blue, monumental and provocative, utopian
architecture, sculpture installation, brutalist
architecture, in the style of paul rudolph, concrete,
contax tix

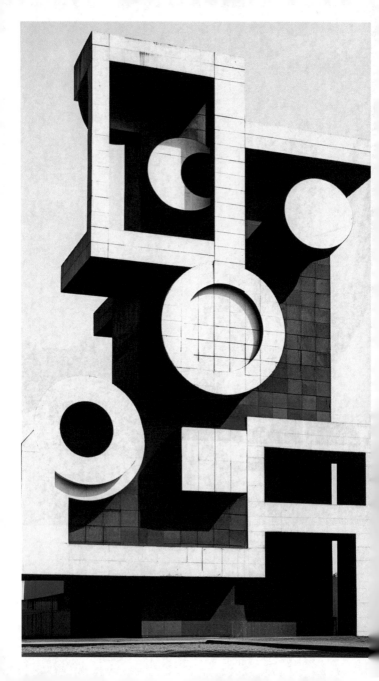

a black and white photograph of a monumental and
provocative ultra-modern sculpture, the support
element is formed by two enormous pylons, with a
circular opening, through which the prismatic body of
the dwelling passes, agustín hernández, in the style
of monochrome geometry, brutalist architecture,
modular constructivism

a black and white photograph of a monumental and
provocative ultra-modern sculpture, agustín
hernández, in the style of monochrome geometry,
brutalist architecture, modular constructivism

a black and white photography of a modern house with one cubic floor that flies on four columns, concrete structure, concrete, in the style of Kiyonori Kikutake, 1958, tokyo

a small abstract concrete structure has been placed
next to a pond, in the style of louis kahn, monumental
forms, interlocking structures, bengal school of art

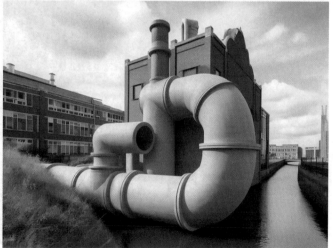

an impressive pip made of pink plastic is built into
the side of a building, surrounded by green water, in
the style of distinctive noses, oversized objects,
pop-culture-infused, romantic riverscape,
industrial brutalist, in the style of fantastical
machines, jeff koons

a blue building painted on a rooftop, in the style
of dutch realism, neo-plasticism geometry, design/
architecture study, raw materials, architectural
transformations, monochromatic color schemes, dutch
landscape, contemporary candy-coated

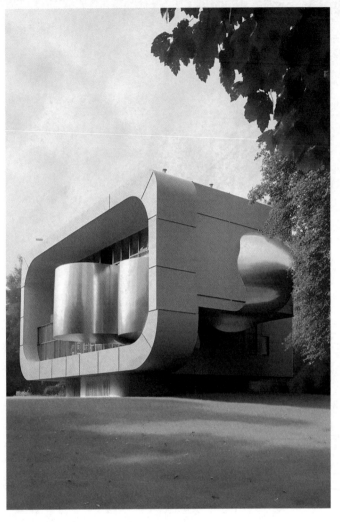

the Villa Savoye be Le Corbusier wrapped in pink
plastic, in the style of Jeff Koons, 32K UHD, grainy,
green and gold, jeff koons, oversized objects,
pop-culture-infused

an impressive pipe made of pink plastic is built into
the side of Le Corbusier's Villa Savoye, in the style
of distinctive noses, oversized objects, pop-
culture-infused, romantic riverscape, industrial
brutalist, in the style of fantastical machines,
jeff koons

grainy photography of the museo jumex in mexico
wrapped in pink plastic, blue sky, jeff koons,
oversized objects, pop-culture-infused, pink and
green, vibrant colors, jeff koons

grainy photography of the gherkin tower in london
wrapped in pink plastic, blue sky, jeff koons,
oversized objects, pop-culture-infused, pink and
green, vibrant colors, jeff koons

⊠ + a pink rubbery mass covers the image, blue sky, vibrant color, jeff koons, pop-culture-infused

grainy photography of the Antwerp Port House wrapped
in thick, pink rubber, blue sky, in the style of jeff
koons, oversized objects, pop-culture-infused, pink
and green, vibrant colors, jeff koons

C 308

grainy photography of the Centre Pompidou in Paris
wrapped in pink plastic, blue sky, in the style of jeff
koons, oversized objects, pop-culture-infused, pink
and green, vibrant colors, jeff koons

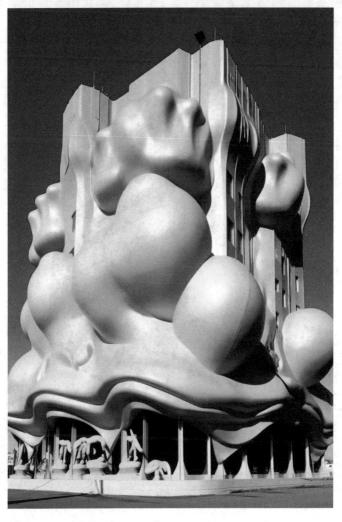

⊠ + a pink rubbery mass covers the image, blue sky, vibrant color, jeff koons, pop-culture-infused, contax tix, green and gold

a photography of a modern building with a melted
golden top, monumentel and provocative ultra-modern,
sculpture, Agustín Hernández, in the style of monochrome geometry, brutalist architecture, modular
constructivism, mexico, post-cubist pioneer, sculptural grotesqueries, golden ratio, concrete, camera
tossing, phoenician art, sculpture installation

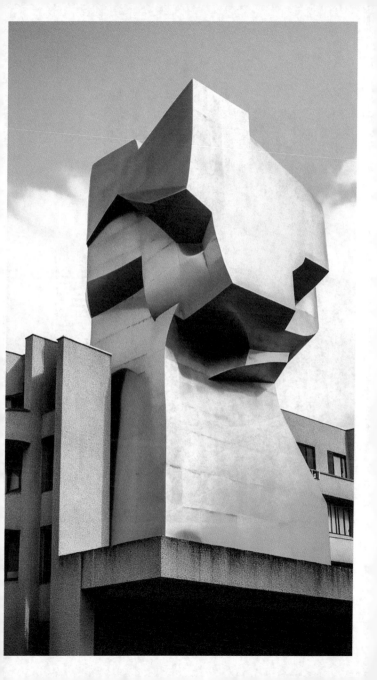

a grainy monochromatic image of the Shizuoka Press and Broadcasting Center by Kenzo Tange with golden sparkles, iconic architecture, grainy, i can't believe how beautiful this is, explosive and chaotic, Metabolist ideas of organically-inspired structural growth, contax tix

a grainy image of Antwerp Port House by Zaha Hadid with golden rain, modern architecture, grainy, i can't believe how beautiful this is, explosive and chaotic, contax tix

the Sydney Opera House is wrapped in gold foil, in the
style of Christo and Jeanne-Claude, oversized
objects, pop-culture-infused, contax tix

the dome of the Reichstag, the new German Parliament
is wrapped in gold foil, in the style of Christo and
Jeanne-Claude, oversized objects, pop-culture-
infused, norman foster, contax tix

walt dwight concert hall at the dwight, in the style
of contemporary urbanism, elba damast, roa,
restrained forms, shiny/glossy, mike kelley, blob,
dada-inspired constructions

an impressive pipe made of pink plastic is built into
the side the Walt Disney Concert Hall, silver and
orange, in the style of distinctive noses, oversized
objects, pop-culture-infused, frank gehry, in the
style of fantastical machines, Jeff koons

grainy photography of the Reading Pavilion in Jinhua
Architecture Park by Herzog & de Meuron with golden
rain, monochromatic, oversized objects, pop-culture-
infused, concrete and rubber, pink and green, high
contrast, jeff koons

this building has a golden tufa for a golden top, in
the style of nyc explosion coverage, 32k uhd, henry
justice ford, grainy, white and gold, spot metering,
high-angle

portrait of architect Alejandro Aravena, realistic,
photography, strong imagery, no background [--c 100;
--s 750; --no watermark, text; --no art]

CHAOS   325

portrait of architect zaha hadid, realistic,
photography, strong imagery, no background
[--c 100; --s 750; --no watermark, text; --no art]

C 326

Mies van der Rohe, polished, steel, glass, marble,
realistic, photography, strong imagery,
no background [--c 100; --s 750; --no watermark, text;
--no art]

CHAOS   327

C

330

Mies van der Rohe, polished, steel, glass, marble,
realistic, photography, strong imagery,
no background [--c 100; --s 750; --no watermark, text;
--no art]

CHAOS

☒ + Ludwig Leo, Umlauftank, realistic photography, strong imagery

CHAOS

+ [REMASTER]

[↑]   train moving around the street, columns and
totems, soviet avant-garde, floating structures,
futuristic architecture, el lissitzky, symmetrical
design

[↓]   russian era photography on the road, futuristic
contraptions, retro-futuristic

DOVE

a cover of the magazine featuring an inverted bridge, in the style of robert smithson, trompe-l'oeil effect, palewave, 1970-present, i can't believe how beautiful this is, seaside vistas, windows xp

the organic design of Alvar Aalto [steps: 50;
seed: 1605576]

[↳]   London Regent Park 1963 [steps: 50;
seed: 8472403]

C 340

Étienne-Louis Boullée sphere [steps: 40;
seed: 3295451]

```
                    DREAMS

                      D
                      R
                      E
                      A
                      M
                      S


DREAMS DREAMS DREAMS DREAMS
          DREAMS DREAMS
DREAMS DREAMS DREAMS DREAMS
              DREAMS
DREAMS DREAMS DREAMS DREAMS
          DREAMS DREAMS
DREAMS DREAMS DREAMS DREAMS

                      D
                      R
                      E
                      A
                      M
                      S

                    DREAMS
```

```
DDDDDDDDDDDDDDDDDDDDDDDDDDDDD
D                                      D
D                                      D
D                                      D
DDDDDDDDDDDDDDDDDDDDDDDDDDDDD
```

DREAMS

D
R
E
A
M
S

DREAMS DREAMS
DREAMS DREAMS DREAMS DREAMS
DREAMS DREAMS
DREAMS
DREAMS DREAMS
DREAMS DREAMS DREAMS DREAMS
DREAMS DREAMS

D
R
E
A
M
S

DREAMS

DDDDDDDDDDDDDDDDDDDDDDDDDDDD
D   D
D   D
D   D
DDDDDDDDDDDDDDDDDDDDDDDDDDDD

Utopia Island by Sir Thomas More, in the style of
keith haring

DREAMS 345

David Hockney, A Bigger Splash, modern house
[--c 100; --no watermark, text; --v 5.1]

DREAMS   349

☒ + Ettore Sottsass, collage, photography

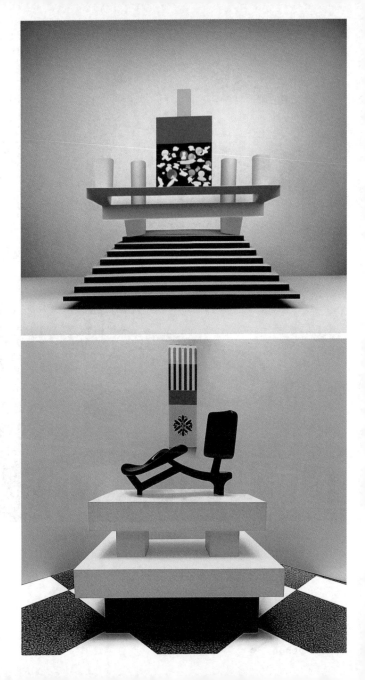

D 354

⊠ + Coop Himmelb(l)au, collage in the style of
Monty Python

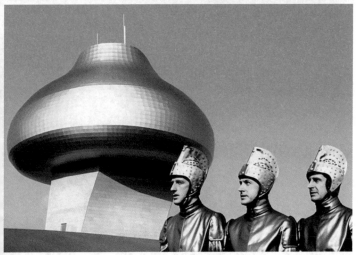

D   358

Buckminster Fuller, dome over whole manhattan,
new york city, photography

[↑]   ☒ + Frei Otto, multihalle, collage in the style
of Monty Python

[↳]   ☒ + Haus-Rucker-Co, Environment Transformer,
collage in the style of monty python

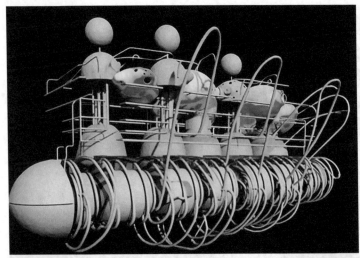

⊠ + Villa Rosa in the style of the Beatles'
Yellow Submarine

photography, the plug-in city by Peter Cook,
Archigram, photography [--no people]

grainy black and white photography of a cartesian
skyscraper, a cruciform shaped tower, it has a
symmetrical form with two axes, in the style of
Le Corbusier's unité d'habitation, Cartesian
skyscraper, monumental and provocative, utopian
architecture, concrete, sculpture installation,
brutalist architecture, group f/64

aerial view of a cruciform shaped skyscraper, it has
a symmetrical form with two axes, in the style of
Le Corbusier's unité d'habitation, monumental and
provocative, utopian architecture, concrete,
sculpture installation, brutalist architecture,
group f/64

we see an aerial view of a city which is divided into
sections of equal size, agglomeration-free
agricultural landscape, one train station and very
few office and appartment buildings, most
transportaion by car, frank lloyd wright, frederick
law olmsted, ebenezer howard, landscape vista,
architecture, utopian

DREAMS

⊠ + Superstudio's continuous monument, 60s photo collage style

[↑|↳] ⊠ + Superstudio's continuous monument,
panorama shot. 4 HD result, cinematic photography
style

D

a modern day old photograph of a train moving around
the street, in the style of columns and totems, soviet
avant-garde, floating structures, flickr, futuristic
architecture, dieselpunk, symmetrical design

DREAMS 373

grainy black and white photography of Dwelling City by
Kenji Ekuan, a diamond shaped megastructure, a city in
a city, 1964, tokyo, utopian architecture, contax tix

D

the architecture of Fritz Lang's Metropolis movie,
ultra HD, super-resolution, cinematic lighting,
beautiful lighting, ray tracing reflections,
incredibly detailed and elaborate, hyper-realistic,
super-detailed, photorealistic, anti-aliasing,
incredible detail, high-octane rendering 8k

the architecture of Blade Runner, hyper-detailed,
ultra HD, super-resolution, cinematic lighting,
beautiful lighting, ray tracing reflections,
incredibly detailed and elaborate, hyper-realistic,
super-detailed, photorealistic, anti-aliasing,
incredible detail, high-octane rendering 8k

the modernist Villa Arpel with its characteristic
porthole windows and a fish fountain in the garden,
Jacques Tati, Arpel house, mon oncle, 1958, bright
colors, in the style of surrealist automatons,
concrete brutalism, playful machines, associated
press photo, de stijl, installation-based

[↑]   The house of The Simpsons, 742 Evergreen
Terrace, Springfield, in the style of Le Corbusier

[↓]   The house of The Simpsons, 742 Evergreen
Terrace, Springfield, in the style of Odile Decq

[↑]   The house of The Simpsons, 742 Evergreen
Terrace, Springfield, in the style of Buckminster
Fuller

[↓]   The house of The Simpsons, 742 Evergreen
Terrace, Springfield, in the style of Frank Gehry

[↑]   The house of The Simpsons, 742 Evergreen
Terrace, Springfield, in the style of Oscar Niemeyer

[↓]   The house of The Simpsons, 742 Evergreen
Terrace, Springfield, in the style of Renzo Piano

[↑]   The house of The Simpsons, 742 Evergreen Terrace, Springfield, in the style of Mies van der Rohe

[↓]   The house of The Simpsons, 742 Evergreen Terrace, Springfield, in the style of Aldo Rossi

the Grand Budapest Hotel, Wes Anderson, in the style
of Jeff Koons

```
                EVIDENCE
     EVIDENCE EVIDENCE EVIDENCE
         EVIDENCE EVIDENCE
                EVIDENCE




                    I
                  NDEX
                    O
                    F
              ARCHITECTS
                    A
                    N
                    D
              BUILDINGS




                EVIDENCE
     EVIDENCE EVIDENCE EVIDENCE
         EVIDENCE EVIDENCE
                EVIDENCE
```

```
EEEEEEEEEEEEEEEEEEEEEEEEEEEEEEE
E
EEEEEEEEEEEEEEEEEEEEEEEEEEEEEEE
E
EEEEEEEEEEEEEEEEEEEEEEEEEEEEEEE
```

```
            EVIDENCE
 EVIDENCE EVIDENCE EVIDENCE
      EVIDENCE EVIDENCE
            EVIDENCE




                  I
                NDEX
                  O
                  F
             ARCHITECTS
                  A
                  N
                  D
             BUILDINGS




            EVIDENCE
 EVIDENCE EVIDENCE EVIDENCE
      EVIDENCE EVIDENCE
            EVIDENCE
```

```
EEEEEEEEEEEEEEEEEEEEEEEEEEEEEEEE
E
EEEEEEEEEEEEEEEEEEEEEEEEEEEEEEEE
E
EEEEEEEEEEEEEEEEEEEEEEEEEEEEEEEE
```

E

EVIDENCE   391

E

EVIDENCE   393

EVIDENCE

E

E

313-347

© 2023 by jovis Verlag
An Imprint of Walter de Gruyter GmbH, Berlin/Boston
Texts by kind permission of the authors.

Concept, image creation, design and setting:
FLOYD E. SCHULZE
Editorial support: FRANZISKA SCHÜFFLER
Copy editing: CECILIA TRICKER
Production: SUSANNE RÖSLER
Printed in the EUROPEAN UNION
Typeface: RONGO M☺N☻

Bibliographic information published by
the Deutsche Nationalbibliothek
The Deutsche Nationalbibliothek lists this
publication in the Deutsche Nationalbibliografie;
detailed bibliographic data are available on the
Internet at http://dnb.d-nb.de

jovis Verlag GmbH
Genthiner Straße 13
10785 Berlin
www.jovis.de

jovis books are available worldwide in select
bookstores. Please contact your nearest bookseller
or visit www.jovis.de for information concerning
your local distribution.

ISBN 978-3-98612-048-1 [softcover]
ISBN 978-3-98612-049-8 [e-book]

E   400

ND